VAMPIRE PLANET

Pg. 124 ☆
+
125

VAMPIRE PLANET

NEW & SELECTED POEMS

RON KOERTGE

RED HEN PRESS | *Pasadena, CA*

Book design and layout by Abbey Hastings

Library of Congress Cataloging-in-Publication Data

Names: Koertge, Ronald, author.
Title: Vampire planet / Ron Koertge.
Description: Pasadena, CA : Red Hen Press, 2016.
Identifiers: LCCN 2015046504 | ISBN 9781597097604 (softcover)
Subjects: | BISAC: POETRY / American / General.
Classification: LCC PS3561.O347 A6 2016 | DDC 811/.54—dc23
LC record available at http://lccn.loc.gov/2015046504

The Los Angeles County Arts Commission, the National Endowment for the Arts, the Pasa-
dena Arts & Culture Commission and the City of Pasadena Cultural Affairs Division, the
Los Angeles Department of Cultural Affairs, Dwight Stuart Youth Fund, Sony Pictures En-
tertainment, and Ahmanson Foundation partially support Red Hen Press.

First Edition
Published by Red Hen Press
www.redhen.org

ACKNOWLEDGMENTS

Most of the Selected poems appeared in collections from the following presses. My thanks to the editors. From *Diary Cows* (Little Caesar Press, 1981): "Diary Cows." From *Father Poems* (Sumac Press, 1973): "I Never Touch My Penis," "Lazarus." From *Fever* (Red Hen Press, 2006): "Cinderella's Diary," "Since You Asked," "Teen Jesus." From *Geography of the Forehead* (University of Arkansas Press, 2002): "1989," "Dear Superman," "Even Ornaments of Speech . . .," "Fault," "Miss American Poetry," "Molly is Asked," "Redondo," "Why I Believe in God." From *High School Dirty Poems* (Red Wind Books, 1991): "Boys from Mars," "FFA," "Frank Sinatra," "Fundamental Group Rejects Nudist Campsite," "Girlfriends of the Magi," "Lilith." From *Hired Nose* (Mag Press, 1974): "What She Wanted." From *How to Live on Five Dollars a Week* (VPC Press, 1977): "I Went to the Movies Hoping that at Least Once the Monster Would Get the Girl," "Soothing the Unheralded Organs." From *Lies, Knives and Girls in Red Dresses* (Candlewick Press, 2012): "Little Small Wee Bear," "Rapunzel," "Red Riding Hood, Home at Last, Tells Her Mother," "What Happened." From *Life on the Edge of the Continent* (University of Arkansas Press, 1982): "Excerpts from God's Secret Diary," "Getting the License," "Moving Day," "Sidekicks," "These Students Couldn't Write Their Way Out of a Paper Bag." From *Making Love to Roget's Wife* (University of Arkansas Press, 2001): "Admission Requirements," "The Art of Poetry," "Baby It's You," "Boy's Life," "Coloring," "First Grade," "Ganesha," "A Guide to Refreshing Sleep," "Green," "Lava Soap," "Making Love to Roget's Wife," "Men and Women," "A Night School Teacher Looks at His Last Class," "Searchlights," "She," "Touring the Creches." From *Men Under Fire* (Duck Down Press, 1976): "Ozymandias and Harriett." From *The Ogre's Wife* (Red Hen Press, 2013): "Hat," "Jack," "Medication Guide," "The Ogre's Wife," "Rumpelstilskin." From *Sex Object* (Little Caesar Press, 1977): "Sex Object." From *Twelve Photographs of Yellowstone* (The Red Hill Press, 1976): "My Uncle Max," "Orientation Week," "The Track Came Up Muddy."

Thanks to Jan Uebersetzig who has read almost everything I've ever written and can still drive at night. And Chris Heppermann, whose high standards threaten to make me a better writer. And the gimlet-eyed Charles Harper Webb: there's nobody I'd rather show a recalcitrant poem to. And Brendan Constantine, whose idea it was to collect the Old and celebrate the New. And always for Bianca.

for the vampire in all of us

CONTENTS

New

VAMPIRE PLANET

SELECTED

Why I Believe in God

I'd failed the examination allowing me to bypass the MA
        and go straight for a PhD, so I was forced to let
my friends forge ahead reading, if possible, longer and fatter
        books than before while I worked on something
by the Pearl Poet for my thesis.

        My advisor was Mrs. Hamilton, a world-class
medievalist and the most patient lady in the world.
        Every week I'd bring her a few pages of translation.
She would smile and correct everything. With her help,
        I finished.

An orals board consists of three members of the English
        Department and someone from another
discipline, usually an assistant professor from chemistry
        who drinks coffee from a beaker. But my guy
was from the German Department. He had a scar, for God's
        sake, that might've come from a duel. He
also wanted to begin because he had a few questions.

        "Vhat was the root of zis word? Zah root for zhat?
Who in his right mind vould mistake zhat as zis!" I glanced
        at Mrs. Hamilton who looked like she was watching
Thumper get hit by a tank. I took a deep breath and replied
        that I knew I was less prepared in German than
I should have been but German was the very next course
        I planned to take. I then hoped to move
to Germany and become German.

He sneered, but Dr. Rosenblatt, God bless him, asked me
        something easy: "What was Keats's first name?"

Then Mrs. Hamilton wanted to know if Whitman had a beard.
        Yes or no would be enough.

I was just getting my sea legs when Dr. Death leaned
        forward. "Vhat," he hissed, "is zah function
of zah ghost in *Hamlet*?" Actually he may have been
        trying to be nice because it isn't that hard
a question. The ghost is the key that starts the engine
        of the play. Without him, Hamlet is just
another pouty prince.

        But I froze. I couldn't think of anything.
My teachers stared at me. They leaned forward
        encouragingly. "Do you remember the ghost,
Mr. Koertge?" asked Mrs. Hamilton. "Yes, ma'am.
        "What was he in the play for?" My mind
was a blank. Less than a blank, a cipher. Less than
        a cipher, a black hole. Finally I said.
"Uh, to scare people?"

        They almost collapsed. Mrs. Hamilton put her
head in her hands. Dr. Rosenblatt murmured, "Oh, my God."

        Then they sent me out of the room. I pictured
myself selling aluminum siding. Or going into the Army.
        Or both. Then I heard the arguing begin:
Shakespeare had not been part of my course work. I'd
        been blindsided from the beginning by
an arrogant outsider. Dr. Hamilton said she knew the German's
        publisher; all she had to do was pick up
the phone and he would never see another word in print.

They called me back in, said congratulations
and (all but you-know-who) shook my hand. Mrs. Hamilton
        gave me a hug and said she'd never wanted
a cocktail so badly in her life.

I stepped outside into the Tucson heat. God was sitting on
        the steps in front of Old Main staring at his sandals.
"Ronald!" He waved me over. "I protected you when you
        drove home drunk, I introduced you to Betty Loeffler,
and I got you through that."
        "You introduced me to Betty?"
        "You were lonely."
        "Gosh, thanks."
        "You don't believe in me, but I believe in you. So I'm
interested in what you plan to do next.
        "Not get a PhD. I'm a terrible student."
        "You're telling me."
        "I like writing poetry."
God stood up. He had a great smile and, except for those sandals, a cool
outfit. "Fine. Be a poet. But don't say mean
things about people in your poems. Be generous. Don't be deep
        or obscure. Try and make people laugh." Then, just
before He disappeared, He kissed me. And that is why I am
        standing here tonight.

Since You Asked

I'd say my style is conversational, or maybe loquacious,
like someone trying to pledge a good sorority, someone
who can't stop talking about her stuffed animals.

Still, I'll bet there's plenty of what people call hidden
meaning in my work. Not that I'd know. Frost's
"Stopping by Woods on a Snowy Evening" is supposed
to be about Death, but it could be about Weather
or Real Estate.

I'm terrible at ferreting out meanings, though I admire
people who can lean into a sonnet with their stethoscopes
and then deliver the news with the same grave expression
as physicians.

For the kind of poems I'm writing now, I'm glad I wasn't
born in Japan. I can see my haiku master fanning himself
as I count the syllables and say, "Two hundred and ten."

No, I'm an American, and a long-winded one. I just go on
like one of those blue highways through Montana with
an occasional joke or simile like a roadside attraction.

Other poets tug on the reins and pause in the dark. Inside
their mittens they count perfect iambs. They think deep
thoughts while snow fills the ruts the sleigh left and
collects on the brims of their somber hats.

CINDERELLA'S DIARY

I miss my stepmother. What a thing to say,
but it's true. The prince is so boring: four
hours to dress and then the cheering throngs.
Again. The page who holds the door is cute
enough to eat. Where is he once Mr. Charming
kisses my forehead goodnight?

Every morning I gaze out a casement window
at the hunters, dark men with blood on their
boots who joke and mount, their black trousers
straining, rough beards, calloused hands, selfish,
abrupt . . .

Oh, dear diary—I am lost in ever after:
those insufferable birds, someone in every
room with a lute, the queen calling me to look
at another painting of her son, this time
holding the transparent slipper I wish
I'd never seen.

Making Love to Roget's Wife

We'd meet in a different cheap room.
Every time I had to swear I worked
with horses and used books to kill flies.

But nothing happened until
we heard Peter from the courtyard
below: "Strumpet, demirep, courtesan,
jade, wench . . . !"

Then she closed and barred
the whitewashed shutters
and stepped out of her only dress.

BOYS FROM MARS

We never get the really pretty ones, just
the runners-up, the girls who know where
the pretty ones are and with whom. But we
don't have to abduct anybody. They run
right up the ramp. An hour or two later,
we set them down with new hairdos
and their shoes on screwy. Then shoot off
to hide between the rings and compare them
to the girls from Betelgeuse, hot as main jets
but each kiss there lasts a year.

And how about the Daughters of the Double
Sun, all ravishing but colder than your Poles?
Who can forget the Maidens from Morbood whose
clothes are steel, or the Big Dreamy Things
no one has ever touched but X19 and he's still
screaming in the hold?

What a life! Prowling the universe and beyond,
sleeping inside cozy cybertubes wrapped
in memories we stole from Heather and Beth,
dear Earth girls right now waking up to
paparazzi and cops, right now saying,
"All I remember is a big, bright light."

Redondo

Beneath my feet the pier shifts
and drools. Above, some gulls carve
out the sturdy air as surfers arrange
themselves like quarter notes across
a distant wave.

It is a relief to stop staring at girls,
to quiet the heart's thick strokes
and calmly pass the man with a truant
officer's scowl, a boy writing a postcard
(that small hymn), and then the great
great-grandchildren of Lady Macbeth,
washing their hands again and again
at the edge of the unraveling world.

What a place to have God rear His
amazing head. Yet here I am, all
the clutter inside made in Your image.
The ocean is forever changing its clothes
to be more beautiful for You. There
is the horizon which You have drawn
with a golden rule and added, too,
a tiny ship and curl of smoke to make
the scene complete.

MEN & WOMEN

When I was five, my mother and father,
Uncle Chris, Aunt Evelyn, and I drove
to the home place near Olney. I stood
in the front seat between the shoulder
pads watching for fires and wild animals.

At Grandmother's house I played outside.
I liked to hear the Savage .22 and see
the fields of blood. I liked to pee
with the men behind the haunted barn.
Their zippers were long as train tracks
and I wanted my little thing to be big
and wrinkled and sleepy looking like theirs.

Later, riding through the dark, I sat between
my mother and her sister, so close that when
they talked the feathers on their hats touched.
Well, not now, she said, *he knows he said it
does it hurts some time have you you do
he does he wants*

I dozed there in a mist of secrets, slipping
from one fragrant lap to another, hearing
underneath the silver fox and gabardine
the hearsay of the real silk.

At home, Daddy carried me inside and everyone
came to watch me sleep. There they stood,
there I lay, surrounded by men and women.

MISS AMERICAN POETRY

At the contest in Atlantic City, my poems
are surprised when a sestina isn't a nap
after lunch. And they're amazed that
blank verse is about anything at all.

Things even get sticky at the mixer. A tall
judge leers. "So you're free verse. I've heard
about you." He leans in. "I have a huge
thesaurus." Up in his room.

On the big day, my poems know World Peace
is the answer to every question, but in the talent
portion, it's hard to see their wisps of irony even
from the good seats. Clutching the Congeniality
Certificate, they fly home.

Meanwhile the local magazines are in the town
square—smoking, revving their engines,
combing their considerable hair.

Teen Jesus

There are a few apocryphal stories about Jesus as a child:
how He walked up a sunbeam and flabbergasted His
playmates, how His bath water could cure any illness.

But there are no stories about Him as a teenager.
Did he make His bed without being told, or was He
the kind of boy who jumped out from behind bushes,
scaring girls on their way to the well, making
them drop those picturesque amphoras.

Did Mary nag Him about outgrowing His robes
and sandals: "Jesus, do You think Your father
and I are made out of myrrh?"

He was probably a cool kid, one the others looked up to.
It wasn't only that He said He wouldn't live very long.
A lot of the guys said that, especially the ones who
drank too much wine and raced their donkeys. Jesus
was different. While everybody else partied by the Dead
Sea, he'd take the rowboat out, step right off the bow,
and sink like a stone. Then he'd swim back in all mad.

His pals could tease Him out of a bad mood, though.
Pretty soon, He'd change water into beer and make one
hot dog feed everybody. Girls liked him, but He wasn't
into them, though no way was He like Obadiah, who made
his own curtains.

Nobody was surprised when He left home. A few
almost tagged along. But they couldn't resist Esther's
long hair pulled back and fastened with an amber pin,

or the pale underside of Miriam's wrist. They got married and never went more than five miles from Nazareth.

When they heard about the crucifixion, their wives just nodded. "I hate to say it, but I told you so."

Moving Day

While sitting home one night, I hear burglars
fiddling with the lock. This is what I've been
waiting for!

I run around to the back and open the door,
invite them in and pour some drinks. I tell them
to relax, and I help them off with shoes and masks.

In a little while we are fast friends, and after
a dozen toasts to J. Edgar Hoover they begin
to carry things out. I point to the hidden silver,
hold the door as they wrestle with the bed,
and generally make myself useful.

When they get the truck loaded and come back
inside for one last brandy, I get the drop on them.
Using Spike's gun, I shoot them both and imprint
Blackie's prints on the handle.

Then I get in the van and drive away,
a happy man.

My Uncle Max

Lived by himself in a little place on Blythe St., not far
from the waterworks. He was my mother's brother,
the baby of the family. I was an only child, oldest
and youngest at the same time.

My mother wanted us both to settle down; she must have said it
a million times. I knew she meant practicing piano or reading
Longfellow, anything but bouncing a ball off the side of the house.
Uncle Max knew it meant some nice girl my mother had dug
up. "But Ada," he'd say. "I don't want a nice girl," and she'd be
just as shocked every time and my father would smile a little
and tuck himself into the evening *Star*.

Uncle Max could do anything with cars. His name was
on the lips of every Chevy owner for fifty miles. He liked
his work and went at it seven days a week, rain or shine,
until one winter he took sick. My mother nursed him
and while she had him down, talked about who would
do this next time because she certainly wouldn't be around
forever and there he'd be in some drafty shack and she knew
this girl.

Mom must have scared him good, because when he was
up and around, he married Iris Wood who had worked
down at the cleaners for as long as I could remember.

Iris took to marriage. She got a phone and sent Max
to the store. When he wasn't eating Del Monte green
beans and deviled ham sandwiches, he dove into the

alligator mouths of Packards and stayed there until
one day he went to St. Louis for some parts and came
back with a woman.

They were out at the Moonlight Motel for almost two
weeks; then I heard that the woman had run off. I
knew what that meant but I pictured her pounding
down the hard road, anyway, with everything bouncing.

Dad took me with him to get Uncle Max even though
my mother thought I was too young. I'd never seen
the inside of a motel room before. There was a bed
with the sheets piled in the middle like the last
of a snowman. There were bottles all over and boxes
of chocolates.

Max went back to Iris and his yard full of cars, but
he wasn't worth squat. He'd lost his touch and his
business amounted to nothing but oil changes and lubes.

My father had to give them money to make ends meet
and once when he came back from there, Mother said
it was a shame what had happened to Max, how he'd
married that good-for-nothing Iris and made a fool
of himself.

My father put the paper down. He said she should drop
the subject. Wasn't she satisfied? Hadn't she done enough?
By God, he never wanted to hear another word about it,
not ever.

He froze the room. He'd never shouted in his life
except for one other time when I came back from baseball.
I had won the game and I said what a nice little town this was
and that maybe I would just stay here forever.

MEDICATION GUIDE

Taken according to directions, Maximinn is perfectly safe and effective.
Well, not perfectly safe. Nothing's perfect. Almost safe. Nearly. Nine
times out of ten. Or six times. It depends.

There are, of course, possible side effects. The most common is not anal
leakage. There are a lot worse things than that. Otherwise clinical
trials would be open to the public.

There may be gastrointestinal events, however. If you are carrying cash
or a passport in one of those pouches that tuck inside your pants, we
suggest you find a safer place.

During cold weather, your toes may hurt and there could be problems
passing urine. If either occurs, tell your doctor immediately! If you
can see him, since vision changes and eye pain are common. Not
common, exactly. More like—well, okay. Common.

Maximinn must not be used by female patients who have children
or may want to have children. Or who may enjoy sex on their hands
and knees. There is just something about that position that renders
Maximinn lethal.

Male patients may enjoy themselves but prolonged use of Maximinn
makes them prone to an oral discharge called Black Throat, so no kissing.
Not that anybody would want to.

Finally, new troubles can crop up later. Much later. Barking and hair
loss, for example. This is called off-target activity and is difficult to
predict. Impossible, really.

Ask your doctor if Maximinn is right for you.

Rapunzel

A story in five parts

The husband: We were getting along fine. I had a good job,
the house payments were reasonable. My wife and I liked
each other. It was interesting to live next door to a witch.
We'd sit out with drinks, and scents would waft over
the wall. Some bad, but some good, too. Slightly intoxicating.
But my wife was unhappy. All the girls she'd graduated
with had babies. One day I came home and she was crying.
"I have to have a salad," she said. "From the rapunzel
in the witch's garden. I have to!" So I climbed the wall
knowing it wasn't just greens she wanted. And the witch
caught me. The thing is she almost looked like anybody else.
No warts, no spindly legs or funny hat. Except she had
a long, green tongue and three breasts and while I stood
there she muttered imprecations and a cloud covered the
sun. I knew I was in terrible trouble. She glided closer
and her voice was like a saw on stone: "Give me the child
your wife is carrying or I'll kill you."

The wife: I've come to understand that I'll always
want what I can't have. And if it seems like I'll get it,
something will happen. It's karma. It's my burden in
this incarnation. Believing this allows me to stay
married. I drive to my therapist three times a week.
We go over it again: my husband is not a knight
or a hero. Just a man with a bald spot and gas. If he'd
died in that garden clutching a handful of rapunzel,
what good would that have done? I am the witch's
surrogate; I carried her child. It was never meant
to be mine.

The witch: I couldn't wait for Rapunzel's hair to grow
so it could tumble from the tower like a torrent of gold.
I longed to bury my nose in it. Stand up to my neck
in it. The smell of it made my ears buzz. We had
fun up there—we'd play mistress and maid, gym teacher
and naughty student. Every skit ended in reconciliation.
Kissing her was like drinking from a golden bowl.
And then he showed up with his royal scepter.
He called to her as I did, he climbed where I climbed,
he lay where I lay, his hands in all her hair. Well,
I showed them. She went where nobody could find
her and he went out the window. Good riddance.

The prince: I fell into thorns and survived, but
I was blinded. There were a lot of princes in rehab.
Most of them were just waiting for their fathers
to die and felt guilty. And I came to understand
they all looked alike, so they had identity issues.
And then there was the dolor of ever after. I
adjusted. My hearing got keener, my sense of
smell and taste more discriminating. When I
found Rapunzel and her tears restored my sight
I almost died from the shock. All those colors!
Now they tell me I'm handsome and happy.
I can wrap myself in golden hair every night
if I want to. But sometimes I go to the window
instead and close my eyes and Rapunzel says,
"Sweetheart, what's wrong?" And god help me
I'm not sure I even know myself.

Rapunzel: Seeing the prince confused me.
Were there other people in the world? And why
were they hairy? His kisses were like blows.
His cheeks sanded down my mother of pearl
skin and the Plough Horse Game skinned my
knees. But I admit he made me feel real.
I was vapor otherwise, only collecting into
the form of a girl when the witch called
and I tugged and she climbed and she
was the oven and I was the bread. I'm
happy enough, and I love my daughter.
But my husband is moody and thinks
of himself. While the witch thought only
of me.

Admission Requirements of U. S. and Canadian Dental Schools

Is your furniture in mint condition?
Has the loathing settled down?
Do you have many commemorative coins?
Do you know what the lighthouse stands for
in poetry?
Do you regard "uppers" and "lowers" as versions
of the class struggle?
If you could snow, would you?
Could you wear a red hunting shirt rather than
the traditional white smock?
When someone murmurs, "But my first love
is the oboe," are you disheartened?
If you were a bird, what would be your wingspan?
If someone said his gums were clandestine, would
you look forward to the drilling?
Do you know what makes bipeds wild with joy?
Could you be specific?

THE ART OF POETRY

My daughter seems to be freezing.
No one knows why, but the tests
run into thousands.

Her teacher brought a book "so she could
keep up," and while it snows outside
St. Luke's, I'm paging

through. At chapter eight ("Weather")
I can hear the siren of a poem
in the distance.

It has to do with this cake-colored child,
the numbness of her hands, a drifting
skiff of a bed.

Staring down, clutching my lucky
Bic, I hardly know what to pray
for next.

Rumpelstiltskin

Music from indoors, a punch line
about nuns, smokers in the cave
of the garage point their doobie
at the moon.

A shirtless boy canters by, his
girlfriend on his back. The pretty
newlyweds can't conceive. He's
grim from laboring

on the flowered sheets. When she
turns, it's slow as a weathervane.
The cranky niece leaves a trail
of Saltines

as she disappears into the part
of the yard held in place by two
dignified trees. Here comes
someone

who wants us inside for an
incoherent prayer and potatoes
white as talcum.

We're agreeable but in no hurry.
The nachos make their rounds.
Somebody opens a beer with
his teeth.

There's a bougainvillea next
door that's red enough to be

annoying. "All right. We're
coming in,"

someone lies. But really we're not.
It's lovely here. The straw of the day,
bushel after bushel of it, slowly
turns to gold.

I Went to the Movies Hoping Just Once the Monster Got the Girl

He was as hungry for love as I. He lay in his cave
or castle, longing for the doctor's lovely nurse,
the archeologist's terrific assistant.

There he stands in the rain peering through her bedroom
window, she in chiffon and dainty slingbacks, he looking
at his butcher shop hands knowing he could never
unsnap a bra

and in comes Somebody Impossibly Handsome
and takes everything off in a wink and she kisses him
over and over, wants to kiss him, has been waiting
to kiss him while the monster feels his own lips
and groans.

I almost shouted into the dark: Couldn't she
see herself in a year or two bored at a luau, another
profile-nobody with his tongue in her ear? Wouldn't
she regret not choosing to stay with someone whose
adoration was as gigantic as his feet?

I went to the movies hoping that just once
somebody would see beneath the rags and stitches
to the huge borrowed heart and choose it, but each time
Sweater Girl ran sobbing into those predictable rolled up
sleeves, I started to cry, too, afraid for myself, lonely as
a leftover thumb.

"What's the matter with him?" the cheerleaders
asked the high scorers as they filed out.

"Nothing. He's weird, that's all."

OZYMANDIAS & HARRIET

"My name is Ozymandias, king of kings.
  Look on my works, ye Mighty and . . ."

"Ozzie, the Thornberrys want us to make
  four for bridge, so stop standing around
  in that pile of sand you call a back yard."

"My name is Ozymandias, king of kings.
  Look on my works . . ."

"Ozzie, David and Ricky just called from
  the malt shop. Do you really owe eleven dollars
  for banana splits? No wonder you're such
  a colossal wreck."

"My name is Ozymandias, king of . . ."

"Ozzie, now the grass is dying in front, too.
  What will the neighbors say? Can't you do
  something besides sit around the house
  in your cardigan all day?"

"My name is Oz . . ."
"Ozzie, don't frown and wrinkle your lip
  like that. It looks like you've got gas."

Boundless and bare the level lawn stretches
far away.

"Even Ornaments of Speech
Are Forms of Deceit"

History of the Royal Society

It's 1667. Reason is everywhere, saving
for the future, ordering a small glass of wine.
Cause, arm in arm with Effect, strolls by
in sturdy shoes.

Of course, there are those who venture
out under cover of darkness to score a bag
of metaphors or even some personification
from Italy, primo and uncut.

But for the most part, poets like Roderigo
stroll the boulevards in their practical hats.
When he thinks of his beloved, he opens
his notebook with a flourish.

Your lips," he writes, "are like
lips."

COLORING

Here is the handyman with black legs
whistling in spite of gangrene. There
are some smiling cows, red as sores.
A jaundiced mare is chewing peacefully.
Two pea-green farmers chat about nausea.

Cute, but no real grasp of the agricultural
situation. And ending mysteriously
around twelve or thirteen with only
the white crayola intact, used for the silly
sheep, a snowman or the rare Klan meeting.

And no wonder! Whoever heard of The Nobel
Coloring Prize. Who says, "This is my son.
He has a PhD in Coloring."? Certainly
no one ever grows up and gets a job
in the Arco Plaza—"The Chairman can't see
you now, he's coloring can't see you now
he's in a crayon seminar can't see you
now he's about to do the barn."

Perhaps some gland does it. Subdued
by greasier hormones, it atrophies or sleeps
as we crouch at the window on rainy days,
every new hair on our new bodies standing
on end as the pillows become the kids
at school we want to kiss or kill, as we
move out of childhood outside the lines
into the real where the sun is not a perfect
cookie in the sky but a big hot thing
like us, threatening to destroy the world.

LAZARUS

After Jesus raised him from the dead
and everyone was impressed, He went on
His way while Lazarus stayed home with Mary
and Martha who put together a little party,
just family and friends, but nice, with plenty
of wine and colored lanterns in the trees.

"Don't shake hands," advised one guest,
"he's colder than a well-digger's ass."
"Lazarus is pale as hell," whispered Uncle Enoch.
A niece added, "Lazarus stinks."

Pretty soon they had him sitting nine yards
away from the table, wrapped in a blanket,
discreetly downwind.

Finally he moved back to the tomb,
going out only in the evening to follow
the sun into the West,

God's name in vain on his cracked and loamy lips.

MOLLY IS ASKED

to be in the Christmas pageant. She tells
me this standing in the door of what we
laughingly call my study.

"But I don't want to be Mary," she says.
"I want to be the guy."

That makes me look up from my bills.
"Joseph?"

"The innkeeper. I want to slam the door
in Joseph's face."

She's eight. I wonder if we'll look back
on this next year and laugh. Or will she
want to be Herod and we'll have to take
her little brother and flee.

HAT

When the final is over, Carlos hands me
something and says, "Merry Christmas.
This'll keep your big old bald head warm."

It's no snowflake ski cap, that's for sure.
This one is the color of quicksand.

Carlos and his friends wear theirs
as they stand in the hall, all their hearts
on one sleeve and that rolled up to reveal
a brutal tattoo.

Now when I go to bed I put on what my wife
calls the Carlos hat. It does keep my big old
bald head warm

and in my dreams I don't take shit
from nobody.

LAVA SOAP

Patient in its little dish, unnerving
in its longevity, this thick ingot
the color of Tijuana jade is still
for men who work hard—
gardeners, butchers, mechanics,
guys who laugh and pass it

along as they get ready to put on
jackets with sneers on the back
and fly across some unnamed lake
toward a woman modeling her skin
like a new dress.

Don't ask how, but I know the Angel
of Death washes with Lava every evening,
then has a hot meal and slips into bed,
both ghastly hands parting the gown
above his wife's quickening heart.

DEAR SUPERMAN

I know you think that things
will always be the same: I'll rinse
out your tights, kiss you goodbye
at the window and every few weeks
get kidnapped by some stellar goons.

But I'm not getting any younger
and you're not getting any older.
Pretty soon I'll be too frail
to take aloft, and with all those
nick-of-time rescues you're bound
to pick up somebody more tender
and just as ga-ga as I used to be.
I'd hate her for being seventeen and you
for being . . . what, 700?

I can see your sweet face as you read
this and I know you'd like to siphon
off some strength for me, even if it
meant you could only leap small buildings
at a single bound. But you can't
and, anyway, would I want to
just stand there while everything
else rushed past?

Take care of yourself and of the world
which is your own true love. One day
soon as you patrol the curved earth,

that'll be me down there tucked in
for good being what you'll never be
but still

Your friend,

Lois Lane

EXCERPTS FROM "GOD'S SECRET DIARY"

Eve has just succumbed to the handsome serpent.
If I say so Myself, I make a good snake. Now she
is about to feel desire. How peculiar to create it
yet be without it, like Thomas Edison in the dark.

*

Now Adam and Eve have really done it! Each gets
an A for contrition, but out they go, anyway. I must
remember to remove the angel with the flaming
sword before Los Angeles appears. Otherwise
people will think this is a car wash.

*

Today I am ambivalent about these particular
manifestations of my Self. It won't be long before
there will be commandments and pathological
introspection. On the other hand, I am a sucker
for sweet talk. Already Eve is a spellbinder.
She is so cute on her knees that I want to answer
all her prayers.

*

It is Saturday night on Earth. A and E are restless,
perhaps dreading Sunday and reminders of what
their shenanigans cost them. Perhaps it is just
the weekend and they feel obliged to have fun.

*

I can hear anything in any cosmos and beyond,
yet I choose the sound of their troubled hearts.
What a funny God I am.

Fault

In the airport bar, I tell my mother not to worry.
No one ever tripped and fell into the San Andreas
Fault. But as she dabs at her dry eyes, I remember
those old movies where the earth does open.

There's always one blonde entomologist, four
deceitful explorers and a pilot who's good-looking
but not smart enough to take off his leather jacket
in the jungle.

Still, he and Dr. Cutie Bug are the only ones
who survive the spectacular quake because
they spent their time making plans to go back
to the Midwest and live near his parents

while the others wanted to steal the gold and ivory
then move to Los Angeles where they would rarely
call their mothers and almost never fly home
and when they did for only a few days at a time.

First Grade

Until then, every forest
had wolves in it, we thought
it would be fun to wear snowshoes
all the time, and we could talk to water.

So who is this woman with the grey
breath calling out names and pointing
to the little desks we will occupy
for the rest of our lives?

A Page from the Apocrypha

So God throws Adam and Eve out of paradise
but they don't slink away wailing and ashamed
like the characters in Italian frescoes.

Instead, Adam turns and says, "Ah, You big lug.
I've been 86ed from a lot better places than
this king-sized salad bar."

Eve starts to laugh, something she's never
done before since there's nothing funny
about perfection.

Adam winks at her and laughs, too.
His hand smoothes her hair. Hers touches
his chest. All of a sudden they're kissing
and looking for a place to lie down.

It's chilly, the ground is brambly and damp,
but they don't care. They're in love.

Not the God-kind, all infinite numbers and
tranquility. But the human-kind, perilous
and messy, the kind that makes you want
to live forever.

Baby, It's You

Poetry lifts language from its knees
in the kitchen, from its tired behind
at a desk full of bills, from off its feet
beside the ironing board, from under
the beater that needs a clutch.

Poetry kisses with its mouth open
and whispers, "Sure, I'm idiomatic,
but nobody loves you like I do."

DIARY COWS

Got up early, waited for the farmer.
Hooked us all up to the machines as usual.
Typical trip to the pasture, typical
afternoon grazing and ruminating.
About 5:00 back to the barn. What
a relief! Listened to the radio during
dinner. Lights out at 7:00.
More tomorrow.

"Fundamentalist Group Rejects Nudist Campsite"

All those oranges, all that warm wood,
grass mashed the way those nudists do,
the stutter of a nudist still hanging in
moist air, a nudist's glass of milk half-
finished in that dining hall, the air
shaped by nudists, lake made to rise,
the dock nudists dove from in perfect arcs,
the tenderness of nudists, the strange
nudist alphabet, the wounds of nudists
healing, coughing of nudists in the dusk,
the unmade nudist beds, a trumpet hanging
from its peg, the nudists' lips upon it, nudist
prayers rising into a bare sky, the stars
burning in the dark like nudists' eyes.

Getting the License

I am causing a sensation here in the County
Clerk's crummy office. The prancing Arabian
stands docile at the curb, the ocelot lies quietly
at my booted feet.

My child-bride looks up at me as we swear
that the information above is the whole truth.
I give my love a ruby for her smile, hand
the unmarried clerk a check for one zillion
dollars and shake hands all around. In each
eager palm I leave a doubloon, still cold
and wet from the sea.

Outside, the crowd Ahhhhs as I throw her across
the saddle. The steed whirls once and rises
into the air. As we float onto the evening sky,
a million children light their matches and her
name appears in flame across a hundred square
miles of wilderness.

She looks down at the speeding earth. "Yes," she
says, "but do you love me. Do you really, really
love me?"

What a girl! I lean forward, spurring the horse
to incredible heights. As the galaxies spin
themselves out behind us, I call to her, "Look!
Look at this!" And then—because she wisely
prefers gesture to emotion—I eat the moon.

GREEN

My mother grew sweet potatoes
in the kitchen window. They wound
around the knick-knacks on the sill.

Her green thumb was famous
and people brought an ailing
coleus or fern from miles away.
She always sighed and said
she would see what she could do.

In grade school I liked a girl named
Deena Vanderwall. Everything
was fine until her mom arrived
one day with a frail African violet.

I saw Deena look for a verandah
and see only sweet potatoes,
oilcloth on the kitchen table,

and my father's boots standing
by the door like tired privates.

Happy Ending

King Kong does not die. He gets hip to the biplanes,
lets them dive by and ionizes them. Halfway down
the Empire State, he leaps to another skyscraper,
then another and another, working his way north
and west until people thin out and they can disappear.

Fay's boyfriend is sure she is dead OR WORSE,
but just as he is about to call out the entire U.S.
Army, a scandal mag breaks this story: the couple
has been seen in seclusion at a resort somewhere near
Phoenix. Long lens telephoto shots show them sunning
by a pool. There are close-ups of Fay straddling
the monster's tongue and standing in his ear whispering
something Kong likes. Look, his grin is as big as
a hundred Steinways.

JACK

After that dead giant gets hauled away, it's just
Mother and me. And the gold.

I buy some new clothes, drop in at the pub.
Girls sit on my lap and tell me I'm handsome.
Then I pick up the tab. If I don't, they pout.

Strangers stop me with the saddest stories I've
ever heard. But I can't give everybody a golden
egg. She might be a magic hen, but she's still a hen.

So I get the cold shoulder. And graffiti on the new
fence. UP YOUR BEANSTALK! And it isn't just
a fence. It's a wall. Which I need because
of the robberies.

Last week somebody snatched the harp. "Master!
Master!" it cried. I leaped out of bed, got off a shot
or two and whoever it was fled empty-handed.

I used to be a thief in that world above the clouds.
The giant's wife hid me and coddled me. Now look.
I'm a fat man in silk pajamas holding a gun.

GIRLFRIENDS OF THE MAGI

When I feel him coming, I start saving
water for a bath. I borrow scarves
and jewels. I eat nothing but grapes
for days because he likes me thin.

That night I kiss his tired thighs,
comb out his beard. I want to play
a game where home is the mole beside
my breast and then he travels south.

But this new place is different, he says,
and fumbles for a map and shows me,
but his finger never leaves the narrow path.

I've been burning like a lamp turned low
for months. Now he says he wants to talk.
Two tents away is someone else who knows
the stars. She says a terrible time is coming.

Is this the beginning of that?

FUTURE FARMERS OF AMERICA

The girls are cute as all get out: ropers
boots edged in cow shit, tight white jeans,
rough hands, and those long poles
for humiliating cattle.

The boys look like tough little fuckers:
sleeves rolled up, belt buckles big
as relish trays, ominous mushroom-shaped
laughs—the kind of kid I was afraid of
in sixth grade on my way home from school.
Another A essay riding inside my Percy
Shelley lunchbox.

SEX OBJECT

She comes home steaming.
She gets into my pants.
She rides me hard.

I look past her slot
machine eyes
to the ceiling

where the last quake
made cracks in the shape
of Florida

and Louisiana, the latter
having for its capital
Baton Rouge

which is located
on the Mississippi,
principal waterway
of the United States,

measuring 2,470 miles
from its source
in northern Minnesota
to the Gulf of Mexico.

SIDEKICKS

They were never handsome and often came
with a hormonal imbalance manifested by
corpulence, a yodel of a voice, or ears big
as kidneys.

But each was brave. More than once
a sidekick has thrown himself in front
of our hero to receive the bullet or blow
meant for that perfect face and body.

Thankfully heroes never die and leave
the sidekick alone. We would not stand
for it. Gabby or Pat, Poncho or Andy remind
us of the part of ourselves that is painfully
eager to please, always wants a hug,
and never gets enough.

Who could go to that funeral and watch
the best of ourselves lowered into the ground
while the rest just sat there, tears pouring
off that enormous nose.

Red Riding Hood, Home at Last, Tells Her Mother What Happened

Like, where to even start. Okay—at the beginning. Right. So I've got the basket of goodies you gave me for Grams and I'm remembering what you said about the forest but now that I'm like safe and sound I can tell you I was totally looking forward to that part. With the wolf. I'm into danger, okay? So I'm in the woods and I hear footsteps or like pawsteps and it's him. And he talks. I'm thinking, "Nobody at school will believe this. Wait till Shaunelle hears!" So first he's all into my pretty this and that, like I haven't heard it all before. Then he gives me his e-mail and some more insincere compliments and the next time I see him he's in Gram's bed and she's like inside him! Wait till I tell Amber that! I am so sick of hearing about how her grandma goes to Cabo all the time and paraglides and scubas. Those things are like nothing compared to being swallowed whole. And it kind of makes me want to know what that's like. So I, like, let him. It's weird inside a wolf, all hot and moist but no worse than flying coach to Newark, but it's not awful and the wolf goes to sleep and snores so loud it's kind of funny so Gram and I talk about when Dad lived with us and the noises that came out of him. Gross. Then we hear footsteps and an argument and then snip, snip, snip we're out! It's this cute woodsman. So we're really grateful and I listened to a little lecture about Stranger Danger which was weird because he's basically a stranger. Then I kissed Grams goodbye and the woodsman walked me to the edge of the forest where he said, "Maybe next time you'd like to see my axe." Which would make my English teacher like light up because she sees symbols everywhere but to me it just sounded like a guy who didn't get out much and couldn't afford cable. So, Mom, is there pizza or something in the freezer because I am starved!

THE TRACK CAME UP MUDDY

and it was cold, too. A perfect day
for a little Early Times in my coffee.
Kidding around, somebody offered me
five bucks for my stocking cap.

The hoods in the box seats are miserable
in double-knits. As something named Big Surf
wins going away, one of them wants to buy
my cap for a sawbuck. All the hunch players
throw themselves in the mud: "Rain, surf,
Big Surf! How did I miss that one?"

Somebody who didn't waves a twenty
by my pom-pom, but I'm busy watching
Louie The Lover who has four girls
instead of a coat.

At the bar, all skin-and-bones buys
me a drink, confides a rare disorder—
if his brain gets any colder, he'll die.
Oh, if there were only somebody somewhere
with some kind of protection.

The wind comes skiing off the San Gabriels.
Everybody shows the mountains his ass,
hunching, pocket-pool, skid row style.
"Whaddya say to a throw at my old lady
for ten minutes with that hat?"

I shake my head at a fifty and look
at the program. It is the fourth race

of a nine race card and getting colder
by the minute.

The sky's the limit.

"THESE STUDENTS COULDN'T WRITE THEIR WAY OUT OF A PAPER BAG"

I gather groups of freshmen. I distribute
blue books and pens, then unveil the bag
big as a bus.

They rush in and I twist the opening.
There is much classified argot, many
contemporary shibboleths, but nobody
is writing his way out.

Still, the bag is moving rhythmically.
There are unified, coherent, and adequately
developed moans. Whatever they are doing,
seems to have a beginning, middle, and end.

"I want to give you all A's," I shout
as the bag develops an afterglow
and damp spots appear all over the place.

TOURING THE CRÈCHES

All the Marys were fine, all with those
innocent necks, but Sondra Knott had the eyes,
too, and got my vote. The Presbyterians
used a real baby and Willoughby's donkey,
even though Sonia Willoughby was a Baptist!
The heavenly hosts were pretty good
but mighty low to the ground and Skipper
Webb, the Unitarian minister's boy,
threw up on all those Glorias.

Driving by again drunk at 1:00 a.m.
on the streets' long rails of moonlight,
all the Magi were home, their beards laid out
neatly on the chifferobes; Sondra Knott asleep
in her sweatshirt and panties; the baby
in the wake of Tonka Town. Only Willoughby's
donkey under a single hanging bulb
like he'd just had an absolutely terrific idea,
one that could change the world.

WHAT SHE WANTED

was my bones. As I gave them
to her one at a time, she put
them in a bag from Saks.

As long as I didn't hesitate
she collected scapula
and vertebrae with a smile.

If I grew reluctant, she pouted.
Then I would come across
with rib cage or pelvis.

Eventually I lay in a puddle
at her feet, only the boneless
penis waving like an anemone.

"Look at yourself," she said.
"You're disgusting."

Soothing the Unheralded Organs

I understand why all of you would like to be
the Penis, who is treated so gently, has a life
of renown, and is rewarded like an only child
who sings, too.

Just remember that the Penis is not so highly
regarded when he sulks, and he is silly indeed
upon emerging from cold water as collapsed
as a tiny spyglass.

Praise, then, to the Esophagus: what a good job
you do, easing every meal onto position. Without
you, other unheralded organs would be hampered
by steaks and chops. In fact, everything would be
knee deep in water like a flooded basement.

Stomach, I know that you would like to work
outside for awhile, slung across me like an
aficionado's bota. I know you would secretly
like to be as public as the Arms and Legs.
But without you, they would dwindle to strings.
They are aware of this, and Hands at this very
moment are holding something special for you.

Old Liver, surely you do not feel left out.
I give you alcohol rubs every evening.

And Intestines both Large and Small,
you are so sweet about a job not highly
prized in this world. Yet you and I know
what a good time we have.

All the Outsides, from Head to Feet, want
to thank you for laboring as you do in such
darkness. With what good will and alacrity
you have performed all these years.

Best wishes for continued success
from the very bottom of the Heart.

SHE

likes big machines. Trains so long
the caboose is just a memory, yellow
Caterpillar tractors that can run over
anything. And she especially likes
those cranes with a big steel ball
that can knock down neighborhoods.

She says if she were an engineer,
she would stop anywhere to let me
on, crush anyone with her tractor
who was even rude, demolish
a landmark so I could see better.

You wouldn't know it to look at her,
to see her eat Thai food or go to
the movies. But some nights the sound
of powerful engines wakes me.

Outside, the streets are empty,
but in the moonlight the building
next door is pale with apprehension.

SINATRA

Every drunk in the world
comes to his last concert.

Frank sings all the old songs,
the great ones, as the swizzle
sticks pile up.

They're so happy they start
to bawl. And then, get this,

he comes down off that stage,
takes off his toupee and wipes
their faces with it!

What a fuckin' guy.

GANESHA

To Hindus, he is the elephant-
headed god. To those who drive
the San Bernardino Freeway,
it is an avenue.

Some of the homes are ugly,
perched on tiny plots, one
lonely sunflower with its face
to the wall, a child on the lawn
with a pan, a mailbox driven
into the ground by bad news.

Hindus would not say, "How terrible
you have the face of an elephant."
Rather, "How absolutely wonderful.
What can you teach me that I
need to know?"

SEARCHLIGHTS

August 1954

For some reason we got dressed up—
to be worthy, I suppose, of the new models.
My father was serious, Mother looked
at the upholstery, I got the balloon.
I remember the solemnity of it all, how
I couldn't touch anything but the brochures,
how cool they were to the cheek and brow,
how I imagined the helium at my wrist would
carry me up and away through a million dying
moths, how the searchlights would follow
me—men pointing, women hand-to-mouth,
the other children stiff with envy—and how
the frantic dealer would have to give my
parents a car to soothe them, something
with whitewalls and a radio.

That was what I imagined. What I knew
was that somehow the searchlights had found
and illuminated my life, and growing up meant
my nose would press against the glass a few
inches higher each year until some August
I'd be sitting with some woman and, seeing
the paths of light scissoring the sky, I'd
cover the tired muscles with good clothes
and talk to the salesmen again, even their
hearts puckered from after-shave.

This poem is in praise of searchlights,
which for years revolved wildly,
pointing in the direction I knew I should go.

1989

Because AIDS was slaughtering people left and right,
    I went to a lot of memorial services that year.
There were so many, I'd pencil them in between
    a movie or a sale at Macy's. The other thing that
made them tolerable was the funny stories people
    got up and told about the deceased: the time he
hurled a mushroom frittata across a crowded room,
    those green huaraches he refused to throw away,
the joke about the flight attendant and the banana
    that cracked him up every time.

But this funeral was for a blind friend of my wife's
    who'd merely died. And the interesting thing
about it was the guide dogs; with all the harness
    and the sniffing around, the vestibule of the church
looked like the starting line of the Iditorod. But
    nobody got up to talk. We just sat there
and the pastor read the King James version. Then he
    said someday we would see Robert and he us.

Throughout the service, the dogs slumped beside their
    masters. But when the soloist stood and launched
into a screechy rendition of *Abide With Me*, they sank
    into the carpet. A few put their paws over their ears.
Someone whispered to one of the blind guys; he told
    another, and the laughter started to spread. People
in the back looked around, startled and embarrassed,
    until they spotted all those chunky Labradors
flattened out like animals in a cartoon about
    steamrollers. Then they started too.

That was more like it. That was what I was used to—
  a roomful of people laughing and crying, taking off
their sunglasses to blot their inconsolable eyes.

A Guide to Refreshing Sleep

It is best to remember those nights
when grown-ups were singing and breaking
glass and someone who smelled good
carried you up hushed stairs toward strange
cold bedrooms to be launched on a dark
lake of coats.

If Memory does not suffice, you may
summon the obvious mascots of sleep,
but forego counting. It is miserly. They
will come and stand by your bed, nodding
their graceful Egyptian heads, inviting you

across the crooked stile to one of those
hamlets nestled between blue hills
where the curious are curious about sleep,
the enthralled are enthralled with sleep,
and the great conclusion is always,
"It's time for bed."

Look—a cottage door stands open. On the night
table is a single candle, yellow sheets are turned
back, and in the garden are marshaled the best
dreams in the world. Lie down. The horrible opera
of the day is over. Close your eyes, so the world
that loves you can go to sleep, too.

NEW

Salt from the Market

The tall woman with the long, mesh bag looks at an array of spices,
each in its own brass bowl, and at the owner eating yogurt, licking it
away from his curly beard.

She likes beards, so she buys a little salt for the tomatoes. He says it's
from the Dead Sea and very expensive, but because she is beautiful
today he makes an exception.

When he asks if she's married, she says her husband is busy
looking for ten righteous men, claiming that if he finds them
the city will be spared.

He smiles, "I say unto you, probably not in this wicked place."
She plays along, "Then I say unto you, we have but little time to lose."

He licks his lips, showing perfect white teeth. And he's burly
with piercing hazel eyes.

She savors the near-blue of dusk while he closes up.
She wonders how Lot is faring. What a shame if they have to flee.
Surely there must be ten.

NOON, OR THE SIESTA

On one of my mother's last outings,
we drove to the art museum in St. Louis.

I could feel her falling away. Slowly
we moved across the slick floors.

The *Bronco Buster* in one room,
The *Passion of Christ* in another.

It was all the same. I was about to lead
us out when we came to the Van Gogh:

A couple asleep, his shoes beside
the sickles. Mom said, "They're not

going to get good silage loafing around
like that." On the way home we crossed

the Mississippi. A metropolis dissolved.
There were fields beyond the water

works—a delft blue sky, and bales of hay
with tired men sitting and smoking.

1948

I was sitting on the floor building a nuclear reactor while my uncles muttered. I had the fuel rods in place and was about to take some uranium out of a matchbox when they said that having sex while wearing a condom was like taking a shower in a raincoat. I paused and remarked, "The simile is misleading on a number of levels." They scowled and summoned my parents. Similes usually meant a trip to the bathroom where my mouth was washed out with Ivory soap. This time, my mother phoned the only intellectual in town who made house calls. He came right over, listened, and said that while I was right about the simile, the steam just starting to escape from the homemade reactor was really more worrisome.

Backstreet Books

Some customers claim the comfortable chairs, others settle
on the floor in the lotus position. One young man lies on his side,
dreamily turning the pages in front of an imaginary fireplace.

I find the Poetry Corner where Frost puzzles over that fork
in the road and Shakespeare regrets his Dark Lady with bitter,
voluptuous half-rhymes.

A fly buzzes, a boy falls from the sky, herons rise and leave
the red pavilion until I hear the clock adorned with three
bespectacled mice.

I am almost the last one out, leaving only a child with her arms
around an obliging bear, the child's tired mom, and the sagging
shelf of autobiographies shouting, "Look at me!"

Super 8 Motel: Fresno

Just a room for a night, much like the inns
that punctuate Chinese poetry.

The plumbing in these walls rushes like the blue
stream beside Heaven Street as a lively
A/C imitates Li Bai's breeze of spring.

The jackdaws in bamboo who tussle, sleep,
then erupt again could be the couple next door.

This morning, camo from head to toe, she leans
against the dusty van and smokes.

We nod. I put things in the car and look
toward the ten thousand hills.

FLASHBACK

Rich people open their carved doors. I eat
the unicorn pâté, then read some poems.

I'm signing a few books when I notice cameras
in every room and I'm reminded of my short
career as a thief.

I fondled the books while the tough guys I ran
with plundered and swore. "Hurry up, stupid!
Get the silver."

I liked the feel of those first editions. I liked
the alarms going off, the sprint to the car,
the getaway.

But with a couple of priors, I was looking at time
up the river. So I split. Moved to LA.
Cleaned up my act.

I tell this story to my hostess. "Really!"
she says, clutching the triple strand of pearls
at her neck, pearls I happen to know aren't real.

FILMOGRAPHY: MARILYN HARRIS
1924–1999

She is best known as Little Maria in the 1931
Frankenstein. The monster throws her into a lake,
imagining she will float like the flowers she'd
playfully tossed there.

It was the pinnacle of her career. Smaller parts
followed: Little Girl. Flower Girl. School Girl.
All uncredited.

Later cheering in the bleachers at a football game.
Standing outside a malt shop with other blondes.
Uncredited.

Her mother turned out to be another monster,
throwing her into a lake of B-movie extras, driving
her to casting calls held by leering producers.

Marilyn specialized in tits-and-tires double features,
often sprawled beside a burning hot rod or dying
in the first act at the hands of a marijuana-crazed
grease monkey.

She'd come home from those shoots still wearing
the off-the-shoulder blouse and smoking, sneering
at her mother who waited on the porch of the tiny
duplex they could barely afford.

AND SENT ON MY WAY WITH A WARNING

When the Salvadoran poet Roque Dalton
was arrested early in his career as a firebrand
and rabble rouser, his poetry was not cited
as evidence against him.

At that point he vowed to never let that
happen again. He wanted to be accused
of poetry and wrote to make that inevitable.

When I am arrested, it is for jaywalking
or daydreaming at stoplights. But I am
inspired by Dalton. The next time a brute
oozing the heady oil of self-righteousness

pulls me over and says as they always say,
"Do you know why I stopped you?" I shout,
"I hope it was for that sestina!!"

POVERTY

My grandfather had one cow. A Jersey. The most valuable thing he owned, and he worshipped her. Muttering in German as he showed us. Daring me to pet her. Pointing one teat at me and jeering when I backed away.

Once a storm came up while we were at the home place. Quick and dark. The radio crackled and then went dead. My mother said we would have to stay. We huddled in the living room with the cow.

Something blew the moon away. I thought of houses made of sticks and straw. Then the thunder rolled east and the wind relaxed.

My grandfather lifted me onto the cow's back where I fell asleep. I remember the warmth and how deeply she breathed.

AD FINEM FIDELIS

Who stole my boxer shorts out of the dryer
at LaundryLand? Just one pair—with the toy
soldiers on them.

Now someone else is in charge of the troops, the ones
who protected me, as my mother would say,
down there.

The thief cannot be as considerate a leader as I who
was always fair and unusually firm.

I miss my warriors. We marched together, drank
together, and raised hell together.

I know they have not forgotten me, and I trust
that thanks to a few hand-picked operatives

that bastard's sperm count is now about zero.

IDOLATRY

My friend who repairs snow globes
has his work waiting for him on a cluttered
table. As he opens a new box of pine trees,

I lean toward the exposed figures who are used
to a constant winter—either a dizzying storm
or days of immeasurable calm.

To my surprise both skaters fall to their knees
as the tiny pond they have been spinning
on forever reflects my enormous face.

BACHELOR PARTY

The beer is gone. The strippers are gone.
Now we're ashamed.

Somebody fumbles with another DVD.
It's cartoons this time. Superman
with a huge tool. Blondie and Tootsie.

Then Mr. Magoo writing love
poems to mannequins. Proposing to one
parking meter after another.

The woozy groom leans on me
as a statuesque blonde leads Magoo's
hands all over

her body. Tears of gratitude fall
onto Magoo's nearsighted bulldog

McBarker, who struggles to open
a small red umbrella.

Assonance

My niece's husband trains fighters. I like to sit
beside him at family dinners. He knows I drove
to Las Vegas to see Roberto Duran, so I've got
some ring cred.

Tonight he's mad. One of his top prospects
got in with some bam bam bam bang
guy and two rounds later he's, *No mas!*

I tell him, "I get knocked around by editors.
It hurts a little, then I think, 'What do they
know,' and I just write another poem."

"Exactly. You shake it off. My guy just
laid there."

Dessert comes around. He's watching his
weight, so I take a pass, too. Then he leans,

"You know those editors you were talking
about? Why don't you write down where
they live and I'll have somebody drop by."

I tell him I like the idea of the muse using hired
goons. And that oo sound is one I particularly
like. I'll remember it when I go to work
in the morning, staring out the window, balancing
my tender chin on my soft, manicured hand.

You're Invited

Another christening. Another happy couple.
And, at last, the building fund's new stained glass
window showing the Blessed Mother chatting

with a few saints. The nuns said those were
sacre coversazioni, with everybody going
on and on about the new Savior.

I used to wonder what happened when the saints
went home and Mary was alone with her friends.
Weren't those conversations just as sacred?

Does He have a rash? Are you learning
to sleep when He sleeps? Is that His first
smile or just a little gas?

Mary could never ask the saints this,
but what can she do about Joseph who's
pouting about that immaculate conception!

Pretty soon it's time to think about dinner.
Mary's friends, just girls, really, have wheat
to grind, chickens to tend.

And grumpy husbands. Babies of their own.
Not as famous, but just as sweet, just as full
of love for everything.

BOYFRIEND

And in from curbside he comes, leaving his impetuous ride all red as
heart's blood, red as the pomegranate Persephone stained her mouth with as
    she chose the underworld like this girl he's come for chose him. So
he braves the cold faces of mums beside the much-swept walk and after that
    a lamp-lit porch and looming there that door with its muscle-bound
lock and nearby the lighted button toward which his eager finger dives.
    Immediately the footsteps begin, heavy as *Ozymandias* on the prowl.
It's the father whose loins once rattled and shook and propelled a daughter
    now waiting, her hair a silken skein, but first there's the tight-lipped greet-
ing, the checking of credentials, the small talk, "She'll be right down,"
    that blessed chord, that shibboleth, her cue to try the stairs in silver shoes
as those below in vaguely air conditioned air gaze up as she gazes
    down and there they are—Dad in his noisy pants, Mom with a plate
of fudge, and he who rose from the slush of other boys to stand out like
    red oxide.

"Hey," he says. "You ready?"

CHEERLEADERS IN THE FUTURE

Sports are enormously popular, especially among
the snipers and the ovenmen. The stadia team.
Cheerleaders gyrate and prance. Their legs are real
and almost all of the rest.

 Dressed in blue and gold, they chant, "Anti-matter,
Anti-matter, you're the man. If you can't do it,
Cosmic Background Radiation can. Go,
Robots!" They shout and toss one another in the air.

Last week, a high-ranking member of the Cerebellum
Cabal was found with a pom-pom shaft buried in his
cortex. But on the night of the murder, the cheerleaders
were all accounted for—painting their nails, worrying
about their hair, talking on what used to be called the phone.

NESSIE

I know what it's like to be a big girl
everybody wants a piece of,

so when another manhandled lass flees
a van at loch's edge, I show my long neck.

I frolic and cavort, turning sideways so
she can see every coil and hump.

Her eyes on mine as she straightens her
clothes, knowing nobody will believe her.

Q & A

Q: Do you ever borrow from other poets?

A: Absolutely. It's not larceny; it's homage.

Q: Critics have said your poems are like Frankenstein's monster,
    disparate pieces badly sewn together that end up lurching out
    of the laboratory and eventually frightening a young woman
    brushing her blonde hair before going to bed. What's your response?

A: Say, that's not bad. Would you mind repeating it slowly?

The Poets' Graveyard

Everybody's heard how aging elephants respond to some
deep tolling of the soul, leave the herd, find the secret place
and lie down forever.

Scavengers pick the bones clean and soon nothing
is left but arcing ribs, enormous pelvis, and precious ivory.

As my gloomy internist probes and scowls, I imagine
lying down in some secret place.

Years later, disheveled men in khakis discover the poets'
graveyard. They're lost, possibly doomed.
But they pass around bleached and tattered pages
and read out loud in voices full of gratitude and awe.

They can't believe their luck. If they can make it to Nairobi,
they'll be famous, sought after, rich beyond their wildest dreams.

CAR WASH IN ECHO PARK

Just me, the kid, and random *vatos*
hosing down our precious autos.

A carvac hiccups, coughs and whines.
With hard work, fenders almost shine.

A single boom box emits notes,
and from our unsuspecting throats

the dark blue of a song we know
rises like a UFO.

We belt it out. Then almost blush,
lean harder on the worn scrub brush.

I call my kid who says goodbye
to other kids who don't reply.

We drive away, as cool as ice.
She taps my hand. "You guys sang nice."

CLAUDIA'S PLAYSET

There it is when I stop the mower to rest.
Part of it, anyway.

And part of her house, too: the window
to a spare room

and under that a small opening near
the ground

where monsters used to come and go.
All around, our houses

are gray and smoky blue. The roofs
are blue and gray.

A crow now claims the scarlet bar and asks
for her who used to

hang upside down and wave back
when I waved.

My Students Want to be Sherman Alexie

They long to be Native American. They're sorry
they were born well and thrived. Why couldn't they
have been hydrocephalic and survived an operation
that was 50-50 at best?

I remind them that Pasadena is a kind of reservation
and they, too, have been lied to and insulted
by their government, just not in the form of free
cheese and powdered milk.

They ask if it's okay then to call their hometown
"The rez."

I tell them, "Go ahead."

Or as the elders of my tribe say so eloquently,
"Whatever you want, sweetheart."

TAHITI

I climbed to the second floor, a place my
grandmother would never see again. A mirror
looked back at me, glad to have something
new to think about.

There was so much stuff. FedEx. UPS. All
unopened. All from my mother and her sisters.

I heard my aunt on the stairs. Together we went
from chamber to chamber. She tried out an ugly
chair. I picked up a box and shook it.

A dress form stood by the attic window.
A vivid print lay across one shoulder and my
aunt drew it, sarong-like, across the modest breasts.

A True and Honest Report about Icarus

He'd lead us through the dark until
there we were, right where the Minotaur
used to sleep!

We'd build a fire, drink wine, and write on
the walls. One night he told us he was leaving

and he showed us the wings. Strapped them
on across his bare chest and the girls
giggled and whispered.

Some say they saw him and his father dark
against the sun. Then the distant one
spiraled into the sea.

There was never a body, not even
a few feathers. Maybe they escaped by
boat. His father could build anything.

That's what we told the girls as they sniffled
and moped. And before long they were
ours again.

URSA MAJOR

The little, small, wee bear pushes the porridge
away and cries.

The other two exchange a glance that says,
Goldilocks.

They know how he feels. Another stupid walk.
Another glutinous breakfast.

"Son of a bitch," mutters the great, huge bear
as he shambles to the window.

He is so unhappy he smashes the glass,
cutting his paw.

It's comforting to be tended to by a middle-
sized bear. Bandage and salve.

He knows it will hurt her feelings,
but he can't help himself:

"Remember?" he says. How she lay there,
he means. Glamorous and helpless.

Waking to Find You Gone

I wonder
if you are like the woman who
made love to her husband again and again

so he would sleep deeply
and she could slip away to meet the young
fisherman

barefoot in pure, sweet water,
the lures he is famous for pinned to his open
shirt.

Contented as I am at this moment,
if I picture you in his arms, instead of jealousy
I feel only gratitude.

La Vita Nuova

I was in Paris working on a rare manuscript:
a cubicle far below the busy streets. Archival sleeves,
white cotton gloves. Pencil only.

One day I fell asleep and dreamed about a woman I'd
met on the plane. Immediately I gave up my grant
and flew to Florence.

I knew she was staying in a hotel near Ponte
Vecchio where Dante first saw Beatrice Portinari
"dressed in noblest color, restrained and pure."

He lied to his wife so he could roam parts
of the city where Beatrice might pass with her friends.
I would do that—prowl the streets until I found her.

In the *Inferno*, the lustful occupy the second circle
of Hell where they are ever restless, blown here
and there by strong winds.

What a wonderful feeling to put on my coat,
step outdoors, and lean into a gale that could
carry me anywhere.

Town Crier

We decide we need one. We've got gas lamps and hitching posts. People get off the freeway for the crafts fair. At first Tom didn't want to wear the red vest and the rest of it. But we figured in for a penny, in for a pound. He looks good, wig and all. Just portly enough. Big, loud voice. Colorful, really. Good sport. Poses with the tourists. Takes the job seriously. Too seriously. We tell him, "Tom, go on home now. It's late." Keeps walking, keeps ringing that bell. "It's midnight, Tom." He says, "Shut up. That's my job." Every hour on the hour. The whole town's awake. There's an emergency meeting. The young men want to grab him, stuff a sock in his mouth. That's a last resort. A lot of us grew up with Tom. Father D'Ambrosio says to pray to Saint Anthony because we've essentially lost Tom. A little late for that, *padre*. No offense. The mayor sends a few of us to reason with him. We're in our pajamas, sort of like the burghers of Calais. Nobody can sleep, so lights are on. People we know are reading. Eating soup. They wave. A lot of us haven't been up this late in a long time. The orbiting moon, not yellow but white as a new shirt. Our wives are at home, so we can smoke. Arnie's hand falls onto my shoulder and stays there. We hear Tom two blocks away crooning, "All's well."

SKY-VU DRIVE IN

First you're sixteen making out
in the back row.

Then you're married
sitting up close so you
can watch your kids
swing and slide, sprawl
and cry.

Before you know it,
you're in an Electra
two rows behind
the snack bar with the dog
asleep on a blanket
in the back.

Stars dangle
just out of reach—
those famous eyes,
the silvery rivers
of their famous breath,
their famous lips.

LILY

No one would take her when Ruth passed.
As the survivors assessed some antiques,
I kept hearing, "She's old. Somebody
should put her down."

I picked her up instead. Every night I tell her
about the fish who died for her, the ones
in the cheerful aluminum cans.

She lies on my chest to sleep, rising
and falling, rising and falling like a rowboat
fastened to a battered dock by a string.

THE INVISIBLE MAN

Failure after failure that made
him vomit or turned him blue.

Finally, success! There,
in the mirror, only the beaker
he'd drunk from.

That headache is gone.
Old wounds open onto
nothing.

He breathes on the window,
delighted with that little ghost.

Somehow he will convince
his wife this is a better way.

Evenings on the porch—
her book turning its own pages,

his cigar like a small, alien
craft on fire.

Jealousy

Toward the end of the year, my wife
goes over our movie list. Most of them
slip my mind, but she remembers
the theatre we went to, where we sat,
what the audience was like.

She's not a student of film—she just loves
movies. In the theatre, she doesn't want
me to hold her hand, much less put my arm
around her.

When it's over most people yawn, stretch,
and leave together, as stunned as Noah's
animals.

She stays, watches all the names: DGA
trainee, gaffer, driver, SPCA disclaimer,
Dolby logo.

On the way out she drags her feet, looks
over her shoulder, like someone leaving
a motel, spent but already thinking
about the next time.

Tyranny

My mother couldn't
bring herself
to discipline me.

She'd say, "I'll deal
with you later,
young man!"

That was it, reproach
that never came.

But might.

The butter knife of Damocles.

Bashful Speaks Up

It wasn't her ivory-white skin or what Doc called
her mammeries. She was new. A neo-thing.

But dumb as an ant. We said, "Don't let anybody
in while we're gone." Three times she did.

Twice we brought her back. Third time wasn't
a charm for us. So we glassed her in and went

back to work. Work for its own sake. But we
knew it wasn't over. Something had to happen.

We're short, not stupid. Even Dopey knew
there was a prince out there somewhere. Sure

enough. We hand over the goods, his clumsy
servants drop the coffin and, like the Heimlich

maneuver, out pops the apple. Kiss, kiss.
Him, not us. All she did was condescend.

Business as usual after that. Sleep and work.
It's wonderful underground: gleam of the gold,

flash of the diamond. Honest sweat, a good meal,
seven close friends, the house to ourselves again.

"AND EPEIUS, WHOM FEW WILL REMEMBER"
—Homer

So Epeius, known as a craftsman,
created a ruse for the Trojans.
A horse for the horse-loving warriors,
enormous in size and beguiling.
Inside, he joins twenty-nine comrades
some dozing, some holding each other.
Subsisting on dates and cool water,
they snore and they fart and are restless
till dawn and the Trojans approach them
and wheel them with joy toward the city.
The feasting is deep-voiced, and Bacchus
makes everyone drunk and befuddled.
Then Epeius, slow-moving and cunning,
throws open the door to the outside.
Goodbye to that hot, stinking darkness.
He is last down the ropes that he lowers.
He waits while the others rush forward.
He pretends that he's already limping.
Above him, the horse blocks the sun's rays.
A shadow falls over the carnage:
broken bodies whose souls have ascended,
a forge with its fire now extinguished,
the shattered remains of some playthings.
He makes his slow way through the blood pools
as Ulysses, the fiercest of warriors,
points down at the body of Priam
and crows that the city is his now.
Epeius retreats to his creature,
the fragrance of wood that he molded,
the belly now empty and silent.
He knows it will molt into nothing

or be splintered and hewn into firewood.
He thinks of his wife in their homeland,
of her breasts and her beautiful eyelids.
Then pockets a knife and some trinkets,
souvenirs for his son and his daughter.

"A POEM IS NEVER FINISHED . . ."
—Paul Valery

Nouns and verbs rise from my lips
and disappear,

a constant stream of them, like bubbles
from a tiny, helmeted diver

who gazes at that pretty mermaid forever
beyond his reach.

PROFESSIONAL WAILERS OF THE HUNAN DYNASTY

A critic for the *Times* reviews a young woman's first book. Each poem begins with an epigram from a famous author. The critic praises the epigrams and neglects the poems in *Professional Wailers of the Hunan Dynasty*. The poet is outraged, drives downtown, and waits in the lobby until five o'clock. When the critic gets out of the elevator, she stops him and begins to protest. "Those are beautiful earrings," he says. "Did they belong to your mother?"

RED

An usherette luminous in white.
Blouse and shoes. A saucy cap. White.

Most of the movies black and white.
The patrons adamantly white.

Her tiny flashlight made a cone of white.
"Follow me," bleached the gloom white.

After the cartoon featuring Snow White,
the hero materialized, hatted in white.

His lies to the schoolmarm politely white.
The horse he straddled relentlessly white.

The lights eventually came up, white
and shocking. There she was still in white

at the peak of the aisle, her white
gloves stained from the tickets. Red.

CONGRATULATIONS

You have been selected. Yes, you. Out of many, you're
the one. Kudos to you. A slap on the back. Kisses on
the cheek and perhaps elsewhere since everyone loves
a winner. Someone like you. A cut above. Nonpareil.
Unique.

Please accept our many good wishes. We on the committee
are thrilled. You are truly exceptional. That is the reason
there is no monetary award. Being *sui generis* is its own
reward, *n'est pas*. These days everyone is rich. What is
a pile of filthy lucre to someone like you.

We are not notifying the news media. We do not
want you to be famous the way everyone is famous.
Your selection by us endows you with a kind of purity.
During the winnowing process, we eschewed photographs.
We would not want to recognize you on the street one
fine day and fall at your feet. Neither did we solicit
documents of approbation, those flimsy ships on a sea
of superlatives. Mere ratification is not for you.
You are not just a corker or a peach. You are not just
the right stuff. You are beyond concepts like *right*
and *stuff*. You are approaching divinity.

We ask only one thing. Keep this under your hat.
Mum's the word. We want you for ourselves. Shining
brightly in our minds only. Should you, however, insist
that a commemorative medal be struck, we understand
and can oblige. Send your check or order for $29.95
to the New Jersey post office box indicated below
and indicate pewter, silver, or gold.

DEATH COMES HOME

from a business trip. He's been gone
for days. All he wants to do is sit
in the bathtub with a glass of bourbon.

He likes the cat to come in and peer
at the water. Maybe test it with one
black paw. Otherwise he wants
to be alone.

Pretty soon he feels better. The cat
is old, so he carries it into the kitchen.
His wife has sent the children
to her mother's.

She asks, "How was it?" "Awful."
"Poor baby. Well, I'm making
cornbread."

He watches her fill a square pan
and slip it into the oven with such
tenderness that he whimpers a little.

Cornbread and beans. If he could die
and had a last request, that is what
he would ask for.

Vampire Planet

On weekends we go to movies. Pay a fortune
for plush, satin-lined seats.

We sip V-8 and bitch about six dollar popcorn.
A medium, if you can believe that.

But tonight's movie is worth it. A robot kidnaps
a blonde. He carries her everywhere.

We are out of blondes here. We should have
planned ahead.

At home, I'm restless. I hate the way some
moonlight sprawls across the children's

playhouse in the yard. I remember plunging
through heavy air toward some lamp-lit

room brimming with smooth flesh. My wife
tugs at my cape and asks, "What are you

thinking about, sweetheart?" We've been
married for light years, so I know when to lie.

"That robot. I feel sorry for him." Her, draped
across those stovepipe arms, him staggering

like a tipsy groom looking for the bridal
suite with its scarlet, heart-shaped bed.

CAT'S AWAY

The mice listen for a cab. When it pulls up
outside, they scurry to the window. They watch
the cat pay, then drag a roller bag up the walk.

They've been scampering all over the house.
But it isn't as much fun. They have to take turns
being the cat.

At last the key slides into the lock. They can almost
see those terrifying claws close over the brass
doorknob.

ELEGY

Poets can't wait to bury their fathers
so they can write about it.

Mine wanted no part of that.
"I'll bury myself, thank you."

I thought he meant later,
but that afternoon he left
a note: *I'm dead.*

I dialed his cell. The reception
was bad at that speed but he
heard me ask,

"What am I supposed to tell Mom?"

"You're the writer," he replied.
"Make something up."

GUEST JUDGE

I wisely separate the cat poems from the dog poems,
but the haiku for an armadillo I keep close.

There's a fair amount of gazing, a moon or two.
Lots of rain and when it isn't busy pouring,
it dapples.

Fathomless is almost certainly on their vocabulary list,
so many things were that. Including a fawn.

Depression makes an appearance in a black cape.
On a windy night. By the fathomless sea.

Then I find "Elegy to a Pink Umbrella." How it
sails away from the poet outside MLK Middle School

but just before it disappears forever, looks like
a corsage pinned on the lapel of the sky.

Deviant Sexual Practices

Nicholas tells me how his father beat him for every
little thing and how that bent him toward the kind
of sex he preferred.

Finding the place was part of the thrill. Somebody
against the wall, posing like a marble sculpture,
somebody else already in a leather cradle.

He was gorgeous and women who couldn't sleep
with him slept with me instead. Afterwards I liked
to smoke in an old-fashioned way.

I liked showing them a poem of mine in a magazine
while I listened to a ball game on the radio.

They'd sit up modestly holding a sheet to their breasts
and talking about their mothers.

If there were men on base I'd ask them to wait with that
and later they would tell Nicholas how cruel I was.

I TRY TO EMULATE THE SAGES

and cleanse my mind. First I banish the moon,
full-grown and warm, then the pure-voiced cicada.

Goodbye to the yellow oriole and the wild
geese, especially the wild geese. Mountain light,
temple bell, beautiful hat, mirror—everything gone.

Except for the young woman in shorts who blessed
the entire *lavendaria* by leaning into the dryer
again and again.

And who in his right mind would want to erase that.

CHARON

It's been a long day on the river. At home, he empties
his pouch. The stacks of coins rise like geysers.

The wealthy who ask for a receipt make him smile
as he washes up.

After dinner he likes to take his rod and reel down
to the Styx. Cerberus wants him to throw the ball.

"You silly pooch," he says. Cerberus fetches,
then romps along the shore sniffing everything.

Eventually Charon picks a few strange flowers, calls
his dog and heads home.

He sweeps his little ferryman's house. Arranges
the few books. Dusts the picture of a girl
barefoot, dressed all in white.

MRS. VICTOR FRANKENSTEIN

She's modeled every nightgown
in her trousseau. Even the sheer
one that made her mother faint.

Instead of kissing her, Victor scolds her:
"A storm is coming. Tonight of all
nights, you must stay in your room!"

Then she's alone with her needlework
and the harpsichord. Again.

The thunder is a relief. She goes onto her
balcony and lets the rain pummel her.
Lightning makes night into day.

She hears heavy footsteps on the stairs,
footsteps that pause, at last, outside
her door.

As that is torn from its hinges,
she undoes a few buttons and pinches
her cheeks harshly to bring on a blush.

$10.00/Hr.

I go in at eight-thirty and read all her notes.
I start with the stains, the black ink and red wine.
Then whites from the colors, like sheep from the goats.
Towels go in the dryer, silk goes on the line.

Clothes tell me their secrets. I know where they've been.
This morning I picked up her pretty chemise
that smelled like a stranger's mysterious skin
and held to my ear I could hear the word *please*.

I shouldn't be talking. I'm not really a spy.
I do housework for money but I know what I know.
I bleach and I iron. Let sleeping dogs lie.
Shirts all on hangers, sheets white like snow.

THE ORAL TRADITION

When he came in for the midterm
conference I asked him why he'd

enrolled in a writing class. He said
he needed something to do at night.

"But I can't put the way I feel on
paper." I said, "Writing isn't always

about feelings. Tell me something
you're passionate about."

"I like facts. I know that's not poetic,
but good old Tyrannosaurus Rex had

twelve-inch teeth. Man, if I had twelve-inch
teeth, I wouldn't be driving no

goddamned cab." "Keep talking,"
I said. "Now we're getting somewhere."

A New *Hardy Boys* Mystery.

We're in Bayport, the boys' hometown.
Dark Frank, fair Joe. Sleuthing
is everything. Who cares about girls.
First and foremost, the mystery:
flickering torches, marks on a door,
a hooded hawk, a crisscross shadow.

Night sounds, shades drawn, shadows
fall across their hometown.
Average citizens bolt their doors.
But nothing keeps the boys from sleuthing.
They're hot for any mystery.
They can't be bothered with girls

though Frank has noticed girls
wearing lipstick and eye shadow
decked out in skimpy mysteries
lighting up his hometown,
getting in the way of sleuthing.
He doesn't want to go through that door.

Thank God! Another riddle to adore:
Now they can stop thinking about girls.
Okay, when they're through sleuthing,
maybe. It gets a little old shadowing
bad guys all over their charming hometown,
solving every single mystery.

There are other kinds of mysteries,
like Ava and Emma sunning next door.
Suddenly it's like their hometown
is boiling over with girls
coming boldly out of the shadows,
teasing them about their sleuthing.

Ava and Emma take over sleuthing,
guiding them toward a different mystery,
leading them into the shadows,
turning out lights, locking a door.
Telling them not to think of other girls,
much less their stupid hometown.

Joe and Frank are stymied. Are these beautiful
hometown girls shadowy doors leading to mysteries
no amount of sleuthing can ever solve?

Saint George

He meets a princess on her way to be sacrificed to a dragon. He has practiced saying, "Never fear." And says it well. George subdues the dragon and tells the princess, "Throw your belt around its neck and lead it into the city." The king is ecstatic. A lot of other girls are grateful, too. They want to touch his boots. They hang on his every word. He explains to them that the dragon is not real, merely a symbol for the Devil. Slaying it means overcoming sin. They say, "No, it's right there. A real dragon." The princess says, "I feel sorry for it. I want to keep it. I'll feed it and have somebody else clean up after it." The other girls say, "Slay it. Then we'll go in the river to be baptized. Our flimsy clothes will cling to our bodies." Their motives are suspect. They've always envied the princess. On the other hand, she is spoiled and willful. A princess is always hard to convert, so it would be a feather in his cap. But he would also like to see those other girls soaking wet. He will pray about this and decide in the morning. He takes a room and undresses thoughtfully. What about self-mortification? A lot of saints swear by it. He calls for a servant and asks for scalding hot water.

Minor Poets

One insists on handmade vellum, another prints in gold
on black paper.

I admire lipstick on cracked mirrors, waiting for the janitor
to appear with his grimy rag.

But my favorite is always the one who composes
only in winter, her hot breath on the cold pane.

Mrs. Mark Trail

Let's focus on Cherry for a moment.
She's taken off her flannel shirt

and rolled-up dungarees to swim
in the Lost Lake National Lake.

A bear appears, but there's really
nothing to worry about. Mark will

save her. He's Mr. Nick of Time.
Except when it comes to tying the knot.

For decades he left her alone to track
down poachers and drug runners.

Then one night as a deer and fawn
looked on, he popped the question.

For their honeymoon they go to
the Lost Mountain National Mountain.

She trims some of her pubic hair
just in case. First she has to be rescued

from an elk stampede. Then Mark
whispers, "You know what I want

to do tonight, honey? Eat a lot
of s'mores and turn in early."

When We Finish the Workshop

and I give the usual talk about submitting
to magazines, my class of senior citizens
laughs. They say they don't have time
for that. They want people to see their
work now.

On Thursday the others head out on their own
through the crowded Farmers' Market. I walk
with Mrs. Rosenstock who is recovering
from a stroke.

The flower vendors get a poem. So does Bill
the Bee Man, and Helena from Egg Heaven.
All the shoppers. Even the rowdy skateboarders.

For a moment as dusk struggles not to give way
to night everyone seems to be reading, everyone
except the lady who sharpens knives.

She does not lift the gleaming blade from
the grinding wheel, perhaps because the dark
figure waiting has told her he is in a hurry.

She Waits

for her husband, the charcoal peddler,
to pack his cart and leave.

She washes away his goodbye caresses,
perfumes her thighs and sets off.

Her lover has a house by the river. He is young,
vigorous and wealthy.

Every passion has its limits. He lies
on a bamboo mat with his back to her.

She knows the poem he is writing. It is about
crickets, wild geese, rain, a dying lamp.

It is like his other poems as she is like other
girls, soaked through by the first bend in the road.

SKY BURIAL

When I was in graduate school, I worked part-time at a local
library. I ran the used bookstore in the basement. The money
came in handy. There was plenty of time to study.

I learned to know the regulars who talked about living with pain
and waiting for bland meals to be delivered.

One sweltering afternoon I read about Tibetan body breakers
who dismember corpses with their hatchets and flaying knives
so the vultures will have an easier time.

I imagined my own body and the monks asking, "What did this one
do?"And the answer would be, "Not much." As the hand I could
have written with flew away from the wrist.

BIOGRAPHICAL NOTE

A prolific writer, Ron Koertge was published widely in the '60s and '70s in such seminal magazines as *Kayak* and *Poetry Now*. His first book, *The Father Poems*, was published in 1973, and was soon followed by many more, including poetry, prose, novels-in-verse, and fiction for teenagers. His most recent book, *Sex World*, was released in Fall 2014 from Red Hen Press. Ron is the recipient of grants from the N.E.A. and the California Arts Council and has poems in two volumes of *Best American Poetry* (1999 and 2005). His books have been honored by the American Library Association, and two have received PEN awards. After teaching for thirty-seven years at the city college in Pasadena, he retired and now teaches at Hamline University in their low-residency MFA program for Children's Writing. He currently lives in South Pasadena, CA, with his wife, Bianca Richards.